The Milky Way
A River of Stars

Suzanne Sherman

Consultant

Sean Goebel, M.S.
University of Hawaii
Institute for Astronomy

Publishing Credits

Rachelle Cracchiolo, M.S.Ed., *Publisher*
Conni Medina, M.A.Ed., *Managing Editor*
Diana Kenney, M.A.Ed., NBCT, *Content Director*
Dona Herweck Rice, *Series Developer*
Robin Erickson, *Multimedia Designer*
Timothy Bradley, *Illustrator*

Image Credits: Cover, p.1, p.3 (background) iStock; p.5 ESO/Y. Beletsky; p.6 G. Hüdepohl/ESO; p.9 NASA/JPL-Caltech; p.10 NASA; p.11 NASA/GSFC/Dana Berry; p.12 Science Source; p.13 (top) NASA, ESA, the Hubble Heritage Team [STScI/AURA], (middle) ESA/Hubble & NASA, (bottom) Gilles Chapdelaine/ESA/Hubble & NASA; p.15 NASA/JPL-Caltech/R. Hurt [SSC/Caltech]; p.16 NASA; p.20 (background) ESO; pp.18-19 (Illustrations) Timothy Bradley; p.21 Wikipedia; p.22 (left and center) Alamy, (right) iStock; p.23 (center) NASA, (right) Giant Magellan Telescope - GMTO Corporation [CC-A-SA]; p.24 Science Source; pp.28-29 (Illustrations) Timothy Bradley; p.31 ESO; Back cover NASA; all other images from Shutterstock.

Library of Congress Cataloging-in-Publication Data

Sherman, Suzanne, 1974- author.
The Milky Way : a river of stars / Suzanne Sherman.
  pages cm
  Summary: "Earth is located in the Milky Way with the perfect conditions for life to thrive. It is one of many galaxies in the vast universe. In fact, scientists are still unsure how large the universe really is--some say it never ends. But with a universe so massive, who knows what else might be living out there?"-- Provided by publisher.
  Audience: Grades 4 to 6
  Includes index.
  ISBN 978-1-4807-4727-2 (pbk.)
  1. Galaxies--Juvenile literature. 2. Milky Way--Juvenile literature. I. Title.
  QB857.3.S54 2016
  523.1'13--dc23
                                  2015003018

Teacher Created Materials

5301 Oceanus Drive
Huntington Beach, CA 92649-1030
http://www.tcmpub.com

ISBN 978–1–4807–4727–2

© 2016 Teacher Created Materials, Inc.

Table of Contents

Our Place in Space

Have you ever seen a band of cloudy starlight stretching across the night sky? If you have, then you are lucky! Often, streetlights, car lights, and building lights drown out this beautiful starlight, making it impossible to see. But it's out there. It's made of hundreds of billions of **stars**, swirling in outer space. What is it? It's a **galaxy**. But it's not just any galaxy. It's our galaxy—the Milky Way.

The Milky Way galaxy is our home, our neighborhood in space. The people of ancient Greece thought it looked like spilled milk. So they named that band of starlight *Galaxies Kuklos*, which means "Milky Circle." The word *galaxy* comes from the Greek word, *galactos*, which means "milk." The Romans called it *Via Lactea*, which means "Milky Road," or "Milky Way." No matter how you say it, the Milky Way is an amazing sight. People in every culture have wondered about it throughout time. We now know more about our galaxy than ever before.

Many universities have observatories that you can use during public viewing times. Observatories have large telescopes that offer amazing views of objects in space.

Billions and Billions

Wait, what did that say? Hundreds of *billions* of stars? How many *is* hundreds of billions? No matter how you say it—a hundred thousand million or billions and billions— our galaxy contains a mind- boggling number of stars. If you could count the number of stars in the Milky Way, it would take about 20,000 years!

Astronomers at an observatory use a laser to help them better observe the Milky Way.

It's no wonder people have been mystified by the Milky Way since ancient times. Nothing else in the night sky looks quite like it. The Milky Way galaxy contains over 200 billion stars. But it contains more than just stars. The Milky Way is also made up of gases and dust. The Milky Way contains planets, too. Entire solar **systems**, ours included, swirl around the center of the Milky Way. It's as though we are part of a giant whirlpool of stars, planets, gases, and dust. Our "whirlpool" takes over 200 million years to rotate just one time!

Because we are inside the Milky Way, we can't see the whole thing at once. Any picture that you have seen of the entire Milky Way is either artwork or a picture of another galaxy. When you look up at the Milky Way in the sky, you're only seeing a side of the "whirlpool." Clouds of gases and dust block our view of the center of our galaxy. Special radio telescopes give us information about what is there. Scientists also study similar galaxies to learn more about our own.

Over time, astronomers have found that dwarf planets also make up our solar system. In 2006, it was decided that Pluto is not a planet—it is a dwarf planet.

Navigation

It turns out that humans are not the only animals that use the stars from the Milky Way to navigate. Dung beetles roll poop balls in a fairly straight line as long as the Milky Way is visible. When researchers put tiny cardboard hats on the beetles to block their view, the beetles walked in circles.

What's a Galaxy?

It may be hard to imagine the true sizes of galaxies, solar systems, and the universe compared to one another. Solar systems, galaxies, and the universe have different scales. Scale describes how big or small something is. A solar system is small compared to a galaxy, and a galaxy is small compared to the universe.

A System of Systems

A galaxy is an example of a system. A system is a set of parts that function together. The moon and Earth are parts of our solar system. Our solar system is part of the Milky Way galaxy. The Milky Way galaxy is part of the universe. So, Earth and our moon are a system within a system within a system!

All of these systems are held together by gravity. Gravity is the force that pulls two objects toward each other. Gravity depends on mass. Mass is how much matter is in something. More massive objects have a stronger pull. Gravity also depends on distance. The closer objects are to each other, the stronger the pull between them. You can think of gravity as an invisible leash. It's as though orbiting objects are tied to the center of their orbit. They can move, but only around and around and around. Gravity won't let them float away.

Quick Class on Mass

Mass is not just about size. Think about a bowling ball and a beach ball. The bowling ball has more mass than the beach ball. Both the bowling ball and beach ball are made of matter, but the bowling ball has more.

If the Milky Way galaxy were the size of Texas, our solar system would be the size of a penny!

Andromeda galaxy

Yo-Yos in Space

Think of an orbit as a kid swinging a yo-yo around his or her head. The string keeps the yo-yo moving in a circle. Gravity acts like the string, keeping objects in orbit. If the kid lets go of the yo-yo, it would fly far away in a straight line. Without gravity, objects would fly out of orbit.

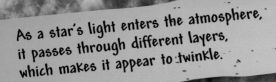

As a star's light enters the atmosphere, it passes through different layers, which makes it appear to twinkle.

Midlife Crisis?

It's true—our sun is about halfway through its life cycle. But don't worry! Astronomers estimate that the sun will keep shining for another five billion years.

Stars

We call our sun *the* sun, but really, there are many suns. A sun is a star, and a galaxy is made up of billions of stars. Our sun is average in age compared to other stars. Some stars are older, and some stars are younger. Our sun is also the closest star to Earth. That's why you can't see light from any other stars during the daytime when we face the sun.

supernova

Stars change a lot during their long lives. At certain points, they give off less light. At their deaths, some stars explode violently as magnificent **supernovas**. Supernovas are the brightest stars. They are millions of times brighter than the sun. So the farthest visible stars may be supernovas. But even supernovas look dim if they are far enough way.

With so many stars in a galaxy, it is not surprising that some of them have planets. And of all those planets, it is likely that some have living things. Astronomers estimate that about 10 billion planets in the Milky Way could hold liquid water, which is an important requirement for life. That's something to think about the next time you gaze up at the stars!

Types of Galaxies

Not all galaxies look like the Milky Way, but they do have a few things in common. All galaxies have a bulge in their center, densely packed with stars. Gas and dust sometimes form arms that wind around in a circle and are called *spiral arms*.

Galaxies can be classified into three groups based on their shape: spiral, elliptical, and irregular. Spiral galaxies have arms that circle out from the middle. The Milky Way is a perfect example of a spiral galaxy. Elliptical galaxies, on the other hand, are almost all bulge. They can be round or shaped like a football. Irregular galaxies are neither spiral nor elliptical.

Scientists are still working to understand why galaxies have different shapes. They think that all galaxies may start out as spiral galaxies. Then, nearby galaxies pull on them, combine with them, and collide with them, changing their shape.

Reading the Sky

In the 1920s, Edwin Hubble found the first evidence that the Milky Way was not the only galaxy. He also noticed patterns among shapes of galaxies and classified them into groups. The famous orbiting Hubble Space Telescope is named after him.

Edwin Hubble

Astronomers believe that when spiral galaxies collide with other galaxies, they become irregular. Over time, these irregular galaxies collapse into elliptical galaxies.

spiral

irregular

elliptical

Our Galaxy

The Milky Way is a barred spiral galaxy. It's called a *barred* galaxy because it looks like there is a bar that rotates in the middle. Stars, dust, and gas form this line through the center. About one-third of all spiral galaxies are barred.

The Milky Way is a little bigger than most galaxies. The disk of the Milky Way measures about 100,000 **light years** across. Its bulge measures about 1,000 light years thick. A halo, made up mostly of **dark matter**, surrounds the entire galaxy. Dark matter is matter that can't be observed but has gravity. Scientists noticed that stars were orbiting the galaxy faster than expected. This means there must be more than they can see. Like all galaxies, the Milky Way is held together by gravity.

The Milky Way has two major arms that spiral around its center. They are named Scutum-Centaurus (SKOO-tem sen-TAUR-us) and Carina-Sagittarius (kah-RYE-nah SAJ-eh-TARE-ee-us). Between the two major arms are smaller arms, such as the Orion Arm. Our sun and solar system live on the Orion Arm. We are about 27,000 light years from the center of the Milky Way.

spiral

barred spiral

Light Years Away

Light moves faster than anything else. A light year is the distance light can go in one year. It is equal to about 9,462,942,720,000 kilometers (5,880,000,000,000 miles). Scientists use light years to measure distant things, such as stars and galaxies. Beyond the sun, the next nearest star is about 4.2 light years away. The next galaxy is 163,000 light years away!

You are here.

 Astronomers have noticed that in the last seven billion years the number of barred galaxies has tripled.

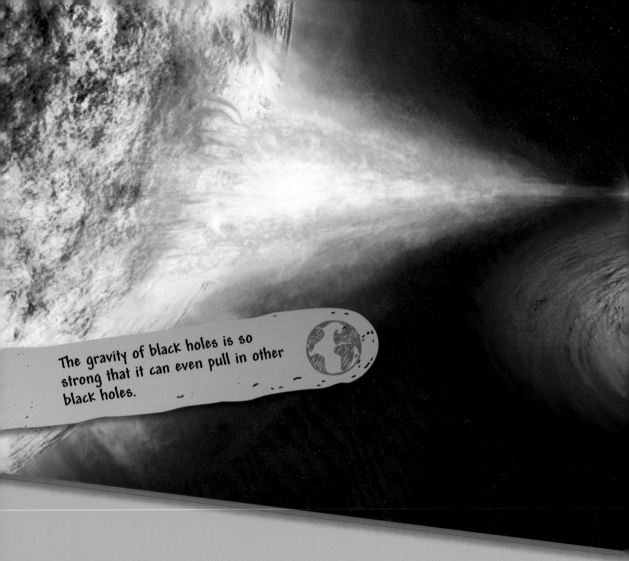

The gravity of black holes is so strong that it can even pull in other black holes.

The Center

In the very heart of the Milky Way, inside the bulge, is the **nucleus**. The nucleus is very dense and extremely bright. Hidden inside the bright nucleus is a **black hole**! Black holes act like holes in space. We can't measure any stars, dust, or other matter inside them. But they are actually packed with matter, and their mass is incredible. They have so much mass that their gravity is stronger than anything around them. It's so powerful that even light can't escape. The black hole at the center of the Milky Way has more than four million times the mass of the sun!

An artist's drawing of a black hole pulling matter from a blue star.

That's Nuts!

Nucleus comes from the Latin word *nux*, which means "nut." A nucleus is the central or most important part of something.

If we can't see black holes, how do we know they exist? Scientists have observed the effects of black holes. They have observed matter being pulled toward black holes. Black holes produce intense gravity that holds galaxies together. Remember, gravity is like a leash that keeps objects in orbit. Galaxies need a very strong leash to keep all those stars, planets, and gases in orbit.

Birth of the Milky Way

How did the Milky Way form? No one knows for sure. But scientists have pieced together evidence to give us a good idea. Astronomers have observed that clouds of gas in space crash into each other and merge together. When gas clouds collide, they stick together and their energy combines. Think about train cars. Imagine that one train car rams into another train car on the same track. They connect and move forward together as one object. This same idea applies to galaxy formation.

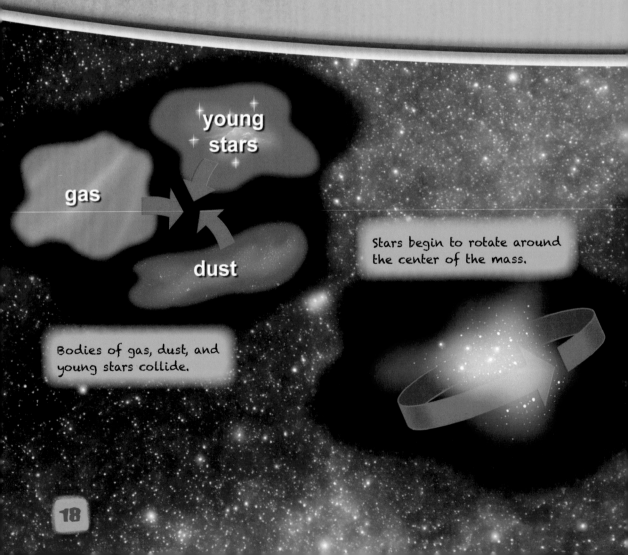

young stars

gas

dust

Stars begin to rotate around the center of the mass.

Bodies of gas, dust, and young stars collide.

18

As the galaxy formed, stars were also born. Stars take up a small amount of space compared to gas clouds and galaxies. And they are not as likely to collide with each other. So where do they come from? It's within gas and dust that stars form. It is likely that stars are also formed from gas clouds. The oldest stars are located in the halo around the outside of the galaxy. Younger stars can be found in the spiral arms.

Nothing in space is motionless. All galaxies are moving away from one another.

Motion created by the spinning disk causes spiral arms to form.

The rotation contracts the cloud and forms a galactic disk.

How We Know

We have learned a lot about the galaxy we call home. It has been a long process, spanning all of human history. But there is still so much more to discover.

Early Ideas

People noticed patterns in stars long before they had enough information to explain them. These patterns became part of their stories, or myths. For example, the Maori (MOU-ree) people of Polynesia had a myth about the Milky Way. According to legend, the Milky Way was a canoe used by a warrior. The warrior took his canoe out on a lake, but the sun went down and he was far from home. The sky was completely black because there were no stars yet. The warrior took his canoe on a river that emptied into the heavens. There, he scattered shiny pebbles to light up the sky.

Democritus was a Greek philosopher who also had ideas about the Milky Way. He thought the Milky Way might be made of stars. But another philosopher, Aristotle, thought differently. He thought the Milky Way was a part of Earth's system. The early Arabian astronomer Ibn al-Haytham (IH-bin al HAY-thum), also known as Alhazen (AL-huh-zahn), measured the Milky Way's position. He concluded from his observations that the Milky Way must be distant and is not part of Earth. Alhazen is considered one of the first true scientists.

I Can See the Light

Alhazen lived in the Middle East a thousand years ago. Alhazen studied the movement of light, the workings of the eyes, and the causes of colors, optic illusions, and reflections. He wrote more than 200 books.

People over time have given our galaxy some colorful names, including the Straw-Thief's Way, Fire Embers, the Way the Dog Ran Away, the Silvery River of Heaven, and the Celestial River.

Friedrich Bessel measures the distance to a star.

Galileo observes the stars of the Milky Way.

Ole Roemer calculates the speed of light.

William Herschel (HUR-shuhl) discovers the shape of the Milky Way.

1610

1676

1781

1838

Help from Telescopes

In the 1600s, telescopes were invented. That changed everything for astronomy. Galileo Galilei (gal-uh-LEY-oh gal-uh-LAY) was the first person to use a telescope to systematically study the sky. He discovered that the Milky Way was indeed made up of stars. His telescope would be considered very crude by today's standards. But even so, he saw many more stars than anyone had ever seen before. The telescope had made the invisible visible!

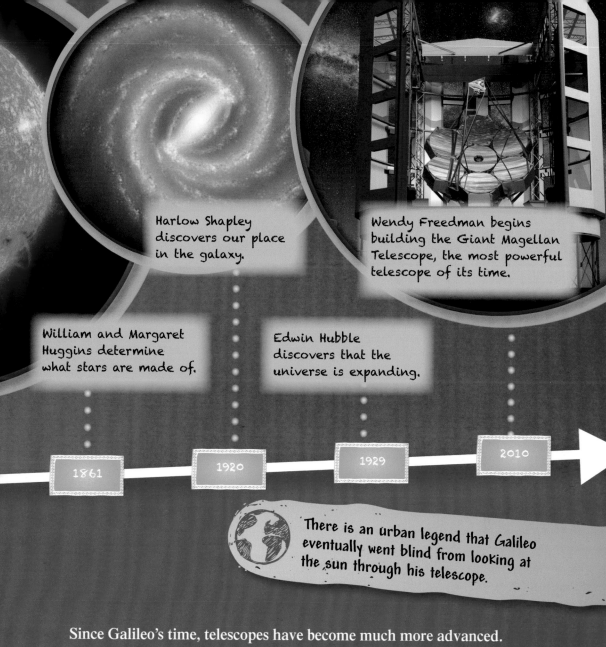

Harlow Shapley discovers our place in the galaxy.

Wendy Freedman begins building the Giant Magellan Telescope, the most powerful telescope of its time.

William and Margaret Huggins determine what stars are made of.

Edwin Hubble discovers that the universe is expanding.

1861

1920

1929

2010

There is an urban legend that Galileo eventually went blind from looking at the sun through his telescope.

Since Galileo's time, telescopes have become much more advanced. Telescopes now use all kinds of light, not just visible light. Some use radio waves, others use X-rays, and still others use infrared light. Telescopes today can be massive. The largest telescope in the world is the Arecibol (ahr-uh-SEE-bohl) Radio Dish. This giant radio telescope measures 305 meters (1,000 feet) across. These complex tools have revealed more detail about the Milky Way. They have shown, among other things, that the Milky Way is made up of gas and dust in addition to stars.

Help from Math

Telescopes reveal a lot about the sky, and so do numbers. Math helps scientists learn from their observations and has revealed much about the Milky Way. In the 1700s, astronomer Sir William Herschel reasoned about the shape of the Milky Way. If the Milky Way is round, he figured, then there should be about the same number of stars in all directions. Herschel and his sister, Caroline, counted the number of stars in 600 areas of the sky. There were *not* the same number of stars in all directions. The Herschels had discovered the disk shape of the Milky Way—all from counting stars!

In the early 1900s, Jacobus Kapteyn (yah-KOH-bys kahp-TAHYN) used parallax to study the Milky Way. To use parallax, you need to observe an object's position from two different places. So, Kapteyn measured stars from two different places in Earth's orbit. He made more than 10,000 parallex measures. He analyzed his observations using math. With this method, Kapteyn discovered that the Milky Way rotates.

Around the same time, Harlow Shapley measured the distance and brightness of stars. Close stars are brighter than distant stars. Shapley made a plot of the Milky Way with his numbers. The plot showed the shape of the Milky Way.

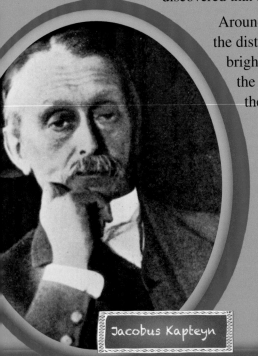

Jacobus Kapteyn

Conclusions You Can Count On

When observations from different types of studies match up, the conclusions are more reliable. The conclusion that the Milky Way is disk-shaped comes from star counting, parallax, and looking at other galaxies, so it is very likely true.

Understanding a Parallax

Hold up your thumb in front of you. Close one eye, then the other. Observe how your thumb "jumps" over. The closer your thumb, the more it appears to jump. This is parallax. Astronomers use this method to measure distances in space. They observe and record an object's location. Then, six months later, they observe and record the new location.

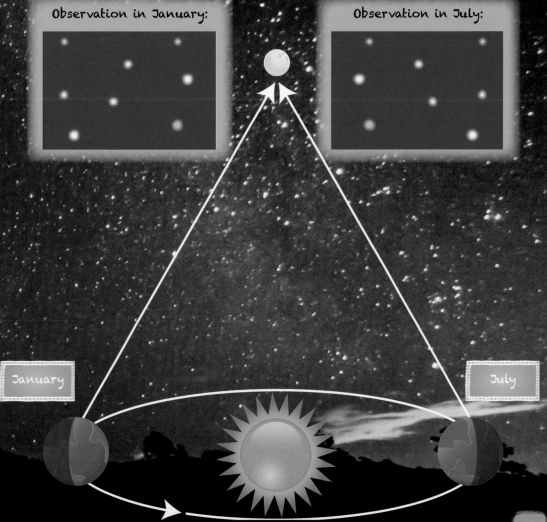

Observation in January:

Observation in July:

January

July

"The sky calls to us
If we do not destroy ourselves
We will one day
Venture to the stars
A still more glorious dawn awaits
Not a sunrise, but a galaxy rise
A morning filled with 400 billion suns
The rising of the Milky Way"

—Carl Sagan, astronomer

The Big Picture

As enormous as it is, the Milky Way is only one of hundreds of billions of galaxies in the universe. Just thinking about it makes everything else feel small. Our whole solar system seems small. Our planet seems even smaller. And people…well, we seem microscopic!

The Milky Way is only one galaxy out of at least 40 galaxies in our cluster, called the *Local Group*. Most of the galaxies in our group are smaller than the Milky Way. In fact, there is another large spiral galaxy in the Local Group named *Andromeda*. On dark, moonless nights during the fall and winter, you can see Andromeda without a telescope, though it's easier with binoculars. It looks like a small cloud in the sky.

Two other smaller galaxies can be seen in the Southern Hemisphere with eyes alone. They are called the *Large* and *Small Magellanic* (maj-uh-LAN-ik) *Clouds*. The Magellanic Clouds are the closest galaxies to the Milky Way.

People have always looked up with wonder at the night sky. Now when we gaze up at stars and galaxies, we can explain more about them than ever before. Imagine what else we might learn as technology advances. Galileo's telescope revealed a galaxy of stars. What might the next telescopes reveal?

Think Like a Scientist

What does a spiral galaxy look like? Experiment and find out!

What to Get

- glue stick
- gold and silver glitter
- pencil
- polyester fabric batting
- ruler
- scissors
- thin cardboard

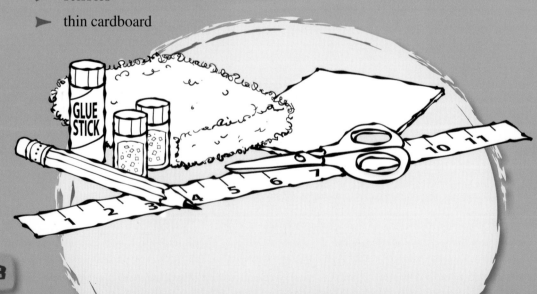

What to Do

1 Cut the cardboard into a circle 12 centimeters (4.7 inches) in diameter.

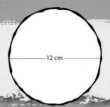

2 In the middle of the circle, cut two small slits about 1 cm (0.4 in.) long to make an *X*.

3 Cover the surface of the cardboard with glue. Form some batting into a ball and stick it onto the center of the circle.

4 Use thin sections of more batting to form the spiral arms. Place these around the center.

5 Sprinkle glitter to represent stars. Be sure to put extra in the center.

6 Slide the pencil pointed-side-down through the hole in the cardboard. Turn the pencil to model the rotation of the galaxy. How do you think this model of the galaxy is similar to the real Milky Way?

Glossary

astronomers—people who observe celestial phenomena

black hole—an area in space with gravity so strong that light cannot escape

dark matter—matter that cannot be seen

galaxy—a system of stars, gas, and dust held together by gravity

gravity—a force that acts between objects, pulling one toward the other

light years—the distance light can travel in one year

mass—the measure of the amount of matter in an object

nucleus—central or most important part of something

orbiting—traveling around something in a curved path

parallax—the difference in how an object looks from two different viewpoints

plot—a graph that shows individual points

scales—sizes or levels of things especially in comparison to other things

stars—huge balls of gas that produce heat and light

supernovas—explosions of stars that cause them to become extremely bright

systems—groups of parts that function together

Index

YOUR TURN!

Observe the Night Sky

Go outside with an adult on a clear night. Slowly scan the sky. Can you see any meteors (shooting stars), galaxies, or planets? Try using a star chart or a smartphone app to find them. Record your observations and share them with a friend.